Miraculous Magic Tricks

MAGICAL ESCAPES

by Thomas Canavan
Illustrations by David Mostyn

WINDMILL
BOOKS ™

New York

Published in 2014 by Windmill Books, an Imprint of Rosen Publishing
29 East 21st Street, New York, NY 10010

First Edition

Author: Thomas Canavan
Editors: Patience Coster and Joe Harris
US Editor: Joshua Shadowens
Illustrations: David Mostyn
Design: Emma Randall

Library of Congress Cataloging-in-Publication Data

Canavan, Thomas, 1956–
 Magical escapes / by Thomas Canavan.
    pages cm. — (Miraculous magic tricks)
 Includes index.
 ISBN 978-1-4777-9057-1 (library) — ISBN 978-1-4777-9058-8 (pbk.) —
 ISBN 978-1-4777-9059-5 (6-pack)
 1. Magic tricks—Juvenile literature. I. Title.
 GV1548.C218 2014
 793.8—dc23
                          2013021323

Printed in the USA

CPSIA Compliance Information: Batch #BW14WM: For further information contact Windmill Books, New York, New York at 1-866-478-0556

SL003846US

CONTENTS

INTRODUCTION

Within these pages you will discover great magic tricks that are easy to do and impressive to watch.

To be a successful magician, you will need to practice the tricks in private before you perform them in front of an audience. An excellent way to practice is in front of a mirror, since you can watch the magic happen before your own eyes.

When performing, you must speak clearly, slowly, and loudly enough for everyone to hear. But never tell the audience what's going to happen.

Remember to "watch your angles." This means being careful about where your spectators are standing or sitting when you are performing. The best place is directly in front of you.

Never tell the secret of how the trick is done. If someone asks, just say: "It's magic!"

THE MAGICIAN'S PLEDGE

I promise not to reveal the secrets of magic to those who are not magicians.

I promise to practice these magic tricks over and over again before attempting to perform them in front of an audience.

I promise to respect my art, the art of magic.

DISAPPEARING COIN

1 Prior to the trick, the magician makes a slit in the lining of his necktie near the bottom. It should be big enough to slip a coin in and out easily.

ILLUSION
The magician causes a coin to disappear into thin air.

2 To perform the trick, the magician holds a coin in his right hand and the corner of a dark handkerchief in his left. Both his hands are level with his chest and his tie is hanging loose.

3 He moves his right hand behind the handkerchief. As he does so he slips the coin into the slit in his tie, then pinches the tie to keep the coin in place. This takes a little practice to do convincingly.

4 The magician is now holding the tip of his tie (with the coin inside it) behind the dangling handkerchief.

5 He raises his right hand so that the coin (which is still inside the tie) bulges up inside the handkerchief. He pinches that bulge with his left hand and lets his right hand fall away.

6 The magician calls for a volunteer to feel the coin by pinching the handkerchief.

7 The magician takes his left hand away. The volunteer is now holding the handkerchief (with the coin and tie pinched inside).

8 The magician takes one corner of the handkerchief in each hand and asks the volunteer to let go. The magician holds up the handkerchief to the volunteer and spectators. The coin has disappeared!

MAGIC TIP!
WHY NOT WEAR A "FORMAL" OUTFIT FOR ALL YOUR TRICKS—A JACKET, TIE, AND TOP HAT IF YOU CAN FIND ONE? THIS HELPS TO DISTRACT THE AUDIENCE FROM THE "BUSINESS" (TRICKERY) USED IN MAGIC ACTS.

THE RUNAWAY NUMBER

ILLUSION

A number seems to transfer from a dissolving sugar cube onto a volunteer's hand.

1 The magician asks for a volunteer to help him.

2 The magician asks the volunteer to pick a number from one to ten.

3 The volunteer calls out the number and the magician writes it on one side of a sugar cube. The magician must use a pencil, not a pen, to write the number.

4 The magician takes the sugar cube and holds it tightly between his thumb and index finger. The side with the number should be touching his thumb.

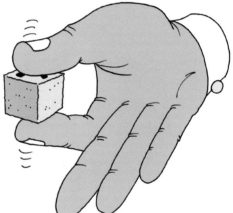

5 The magician drops the sugar cube into a glass of cold water.

6 He takes the volunteer's hand, palm up, and holds it over the glass. The magician must be sure to press his thumb firmly against the volunteer's hand.

7 As the sugar cube dissolves, the magician says that the number has magically transferred onto the volunteer's hand. The magician releases the volunteer's hand. He asks the volunteer to show her palm to the audience. The number is clearly visible on it!

VANISHING MARBLE

1 Prior to the trick, the magician cuts a hole in the bottom of a paper cup. The hole must be big enough for a marble to pass through.

ILLUSION

A marble dropped into a paper cup disappears— then reappears from inside the magician's pocket!

2 The magician puts a marble (identical to the one he'll be using in the trick) into his right-hand jacket pocket.

3 The magician begins the trick by holding the paper cup in his left hand. His hand forms a bowl beneath the cup.

4 He holds a marble in his right hand and says he will make it disappear.

5 He drops the marble into the cup. It passes through the hole and lands in his left palm.

6 The magician tilts his left hand so that the marble rolls a little.

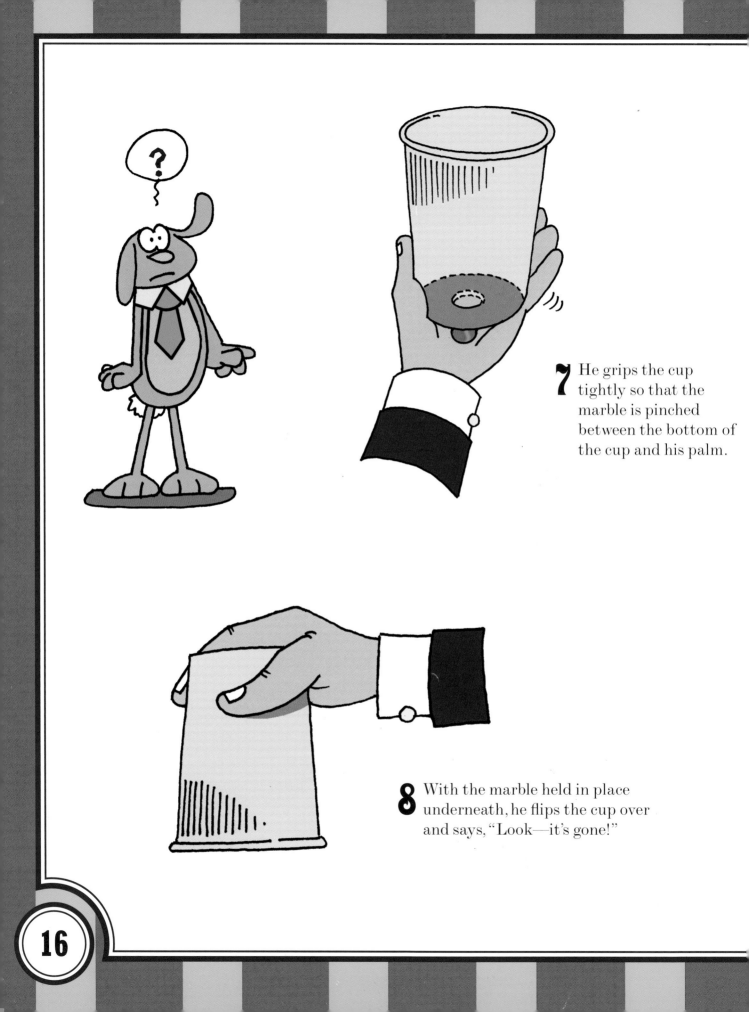

7 He grips the cup tightly so that the marble is pinched between the bottom of the cup and his palm.

8 With the marble held in place underneath, he flips the cup over and says, "Look—it's gone!"

9 The magician lowers his left hand, saying: "Wait! Here it is!" With his right hand he reaches into his pocket and pulls out the spare marble.

10 He passes the marble round for the spectators to check, and puts the cup and the other marble out of sight.

ESCAPING COIN

1 The magician holds holds a coin by the edges between the thumb and third finger of his left hand.

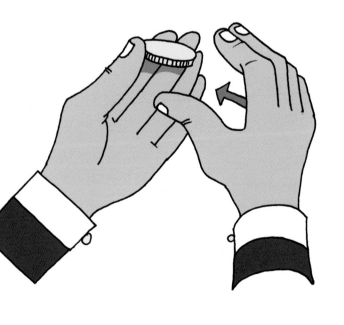

2 He pretends to grab the coin by moving his right hand towards it.

18

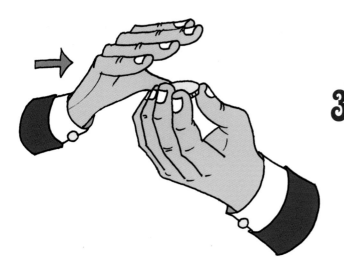

3 His right thumb passes under the coin and his fingers pass above it. The coin is covered by his right hand.

4 The magician makes a fist with his right hand and pulls it away. But he simply pulls away an empty fist. He allows the coin to drop into his left palm. He lets his left hand "go dead" by dropping it down with its back to the audience. The spectators think the coin is in his right hand.

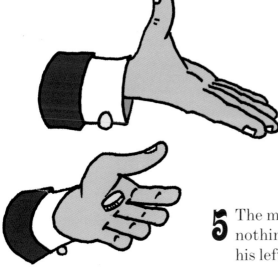

5 The magician opens his right hand. There's nothing there! Then he straightens the fingers of his left hand to reveal the coin back there again.

WHO'S WATCHING THE WATCH?

1 Prior to the trick, the magician secretly chooses a partner who will be in on the trick.

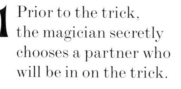

2 The partner sits in the audience.

3 The magician begins the trick by asking to borrow a spectator's watch.

4 The magician takes the watch in his right hand. He flips his hand over and covers it with a dark handkerchief.

5 The magician gets the spectators to come up and feel the watch under the handkerchief. (The partner waits for the others to go, then goes up last.)

6 As the partner approaches, the magician waves his left hand slowly to distract the spectators. He widens his eyes and says, "This trick even fooled the great Houdini!" While the magician is saying this, the partner grasps the wristwatch and hides it in his clenched fist. He walks back to his seat.

7 The magician whisks the handkerchief away. He opens his hand—the watch has disappeared!

GOOFY GRAPES

1 The magician performs this trick while seated behind a table. He has hidden one grape in his lap and set three others on the table.

ILLUSION
The magician makes several grapes disappear—and reappear just as quickly!

2 He begins by saying, "I'm going to get rid of one grape." He picks up a grape with his left hand and drops his hand behind the table. Spectators think he's dropped the grape.

3 But he has held onto the grape and picked up the hidden grape. He hides the two grapes in three curved fingers as he brings his hand back up.

4 "Right. Now there are two," he says. In sight of the audience, he picks up a second grape from the table (still hiding the two grapes he is holding).

5 The magician puts all three grapes (the hidden two plus the one he has just picked up) into his right hand beneath the table. He does this quickly and closes his hand. The audience thinks he has one grape in his left hand, thrown one away and still has one on the table.

6 "OK," he says, "Let's get rid of the last one." This time he really does push the remaining grape into his lap.

7 He finishes by saying: "So that leaves one, two, three grapes on the table." He counts the hidden grapes out from his right hand.

ELASTIC BAND JUMP

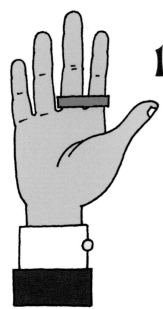

1 The magician places an elastic band over the index and middle fingers of his right hand. The back of his hand is facing the audience. He pulls the band down to the base of his fingers.

ILLUSION

An elastic band jumps from two of the magician's fingers to another two—without touching anything.

2 Now the magician walks among the spectators, asking them to pull on the band to make sure it's real.

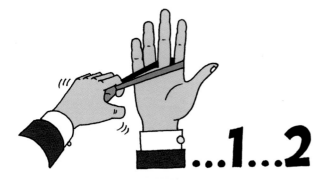

...1...2

3 The magician holds his right hand up again, as he did at the start of the trick. He says that on the count of three he will make the band jump along his hand to the last two fingers. He pulls back the band, releases it and says "One." He does the same on the count of "Two."

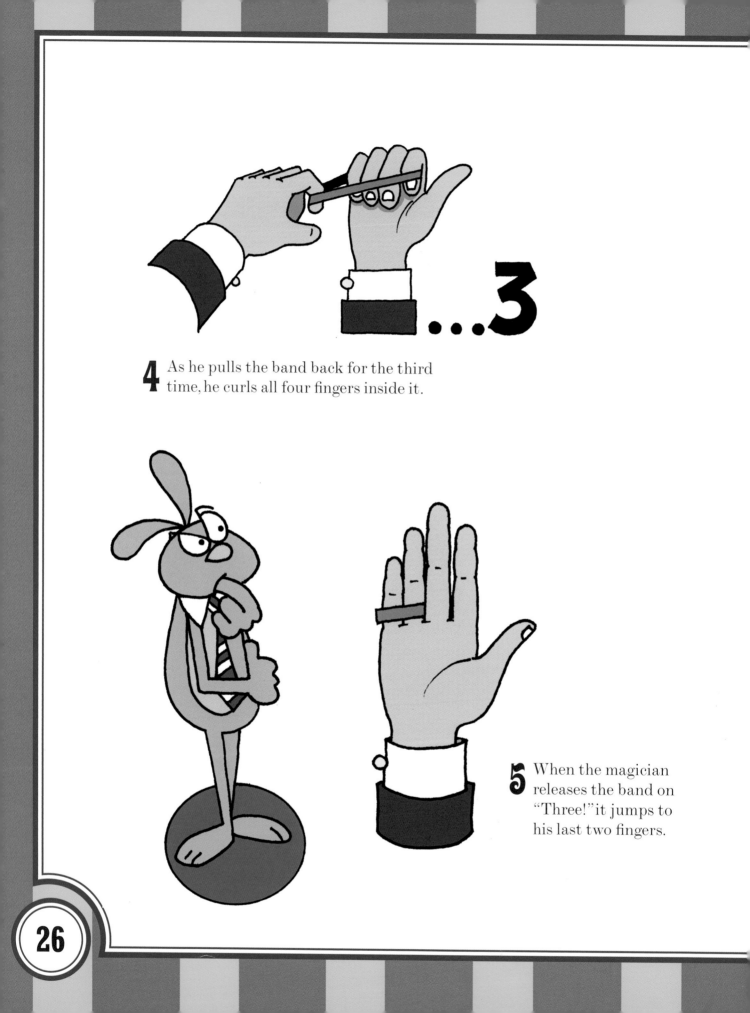

4 As he pulls the band back for the third time, he curls all four fingers inside it.

5 When the magician releases the band on "Three!" it jumps to his last two fingers.

TOOTHPICK TRICKERY

1 Prior to the trick, the magician uses a piece of clear tape to stick a toothpick to his right thumbnail. The toothpick should not jut out over the top of the thumb.

2 The magician gets the toothpick in position by covering his thumbnail with his index finger and bending his thumb. With enough bending, the toothpick will stand up nearly straight. To perform the trick, the magician says he can make the toothpick disappear with a single wave of his hand.

3 He asks the spectators to watch closely as he does the trick. The magician swipes his left hand in front of his right hand. As it passes, he straightens his thumb, so that the toothpick is concealed.

4 The magician holds up his hands to the audience, who can't see the toothpick because it is nestled behind his thumb.

MAGIC TIP
THE MAGICIAN CAN MAKE THE TOOTHPICK REAPPEAR BY BENDING HIS RIGHT THUMB AS HIS LEFT HAND PASSES BACK OVER IT.

THIMBLE MYSTERY

1 Prior to the trick, the magician makes sure the side pockets of his jacket are open so that he can drop things into them quickly. To perform the trick, the magician tells his spectators that he will use an ordinary pencil as a wand to help him make something disappear. He will start with something small—like a thimble. He holds the pencil in his right hand and the thimble in his left. He closes his fist over the thimble.

ILLUSION

The magician magically makes a thimble disappear.

ONE...

2 He reminds the spectators that it takes three taps of the wand to make the trick work. He raises the pencil until it is just behind his right ear. Then, on the count of "ONE," he swings the pencil down and taps his closed left hand.

TWO...

3 The magician then raises the pencil to his right ear again. On the count of "TWO," he swings it down and taps his left hand again.

4 He raises the pencil once more, but this time rests it behind his right ear. On the count of "THREE," he extends his index finger and swings it down (just as he did with the pencil). He holds up his right hand and says, "Whoops—I've made the wrong thing disappear!"

5 The magician continues to look at his right hand. When someone shouts: "It's behind your ear," he flutters his right hand and goes to grab the pencil.

6 He makes a fuss about yanking the pencil from behind his ear, saying: "I hope it's not stuck!" He even twists his body a little to give the spectators a better view of his fumbling. As he distracts the spectators in this way, he secretly moves his left hand back and lets the thimble drop into his jacket pocket. He keeps his left hand clenched and raises it again.

7 The magician finishes by saying he still thought the trick worked. He opens his left hand—and there's no thimble!

FURTHER READING

Barnhart, Norm. *Amazing Magic Tricks.* Mankato, MN: Capstone Press, 2009.

Cassidy, John and Michael Stroud. *Klutz Book of Magic.* Palo Alto, CA: Klutz Press, 2006.

Charney, Steve. *Cool Card Tricks.* Easy Magic Tricks. Mankato, MN: Capstone Press, 2010.

Klingel, Cynthia and Robert B. Noyed. *Card Tricks.* Games Around the World. Mankato, MN: Compass Point Books, 2002.

Longe, Bob. *The Little Giant Book of Card Tricks.* New York: Sterling Publishers Inc, 2000.

WEBSITES

For web resources related to the subject of this book, go to: www.windmillbooks.com/weblinks and select this book's title.

GLOSSARY

convincingly (kun-VIN-sing-lee) In a way that looks real.

dissolve (dih-ZOLV) To become part of a liquid when mixed with a liquid.

index finger (IN-deks FING-gur) The finger next to the thumb.

level (LEH-vuhl) At the same height.

sleight of hand (SLYT UV HAND) Moving your hands in a sneaky way to confuse the audience.

spectator (SPEK-tay-ter) A person who sees or watches something.

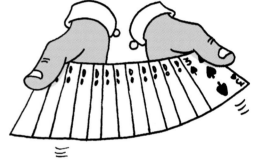

INDEX